AF412032

I believe

by Bob B. Ashton
Photographs by Alan Fontaine
Designed by Ron Gilbert

The C. R. Gibson Company, *Publishers*
Norwalk, Connecticut

The Dawning of a Better Day

The sun that sets far in the west
   proclaiming night's repose,
Continues on to other lands
   new brightness to disclose . . .
The same is true from mortal view
   when life is passing on,
For what appears as earthly night
   becomes another dawn . . .

But as it is written, Eye hath not seen, nor ear heard,
neither have entered into the heart of man, the things
which God hath prepared for them that love him.

I Corinthians 2:9

Copyright MCMLXXIV by
The C. R. Gibson Company, Norwalk, Connecticut
All rights reserved
Printed in the United States of America
Library of Congress Catalog Card Number: 74-83773
ISBN: 0-8378-2007-3

The Vantage Point

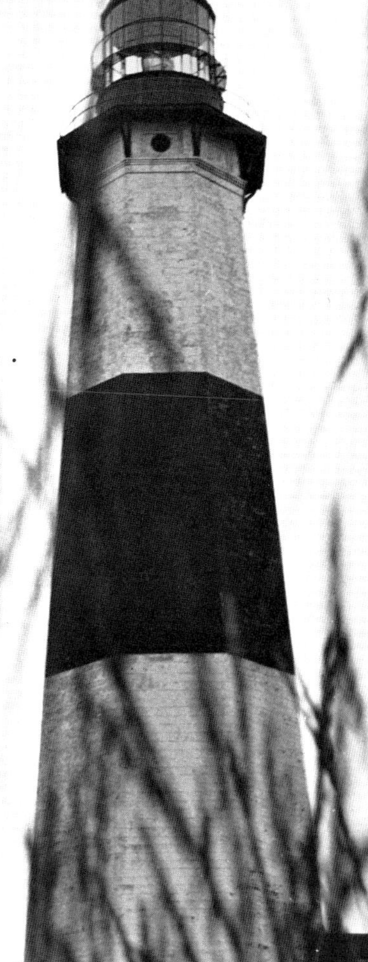

From where I sit
the day looks bleak . . .
My senses cry out "doom"!
Oppressing clouds
of darkest gray
add misery to the gloom . . .
Were I to seek
the mortal mind,
despair would fill my heart.
But long ago
I've learned to view
the whole and not the part . . .
For He Who guides
my every step
with vision unimpaired,
has given promise
in His Word
that I've been fully spared!

And we know that all things
work together for good to them
that love God, who are the
called according to His purpose.
Romans 8:28

He's My Savior

He's the King of all Kings,
unto Him my heart sings . . .
Perfect Brother,
like no other,
He's my Saviour . . .
He's the Author of Grace,
for the whole human race . . .
Ev'ry nation
His creation
of love . . .
Were the things of this world
all my own,
I would rather have Jesus
alone . . .
He's my pardon from sin,
as it's pledg'd to all men . . .
Source of power,
every hour,
as I need Him . . .
And forever I'll claim
promises in His Name . . .
Perfect union,
my communion
with God.

But we see Jesus, who was made a little lower than the angels for the suffering of death, crowned with glory and honour; that he by the grace of God should taste death for every man. For it became him, for whom are all things, and by whom are all things, in bringing many sons unto glory, to make the captain of their salvation perfect through sufferings.

Hebrews 2: 9 & 10

Goodbye

It's not a task to brave the deep
   Nor face the darken'd sky,
But strength has ne'er been known to man
   To eas'ly say "goodbye".

Sorrow is better than laughter: for by the sadness of
the countenance the heart is made better.
Ecclesiastes 7:3

Hello

No ear hath heard a sweeter sound
   To set the world aglow
Than that response when eyes have met
   And two hearts say "hello".

O magnify the Lord with me, and let us exalt his name
together.   *Psalm 34:3*

Storms of Life

In troubled times when days seem dark
   and hope begins to dim,
Resort no more to earthly aid
   but cast your care on Him . . .
For winds that storm across the land
   and cause much tribulation,
Bring also rain and seas'nal change
   as part of God's creation . . .

And who is he that will harm you, if ye be followers
of that which is good?   *I Peter 3:13*

The Key To Faith

For now we do not falter
when faith is but our grasp;
For what we see
shows not the key . . .
It's in WHOSE HAND we clasp.

Now faith is the substance of things hoped for, the
evidence of things not seen.   *Hebrews 11:1*

Kingship

A man once wore a robe and crown
and swore his kingship real . . .
His voice in great majestic tones
gave vent to mass appeal.
But soon the farce was known by all
for kings must gain control . . .
And this poor man had failed to rule
the kingdom of his soul.

He that hath no rule over his own spirit is like a city
that is broken down, and without walls.
        Proverbs 25:28

The Mainstream

I watch'd the lazy stream go by
and thought, it barely flows!
Perhaps it has no destiny
and cares not where it goes . . .
But such is not the case I find,
for underneath this mask,
a vibrant force is well at work
accomplishing its task.

But let judgement run
down as waters, and
righteousness as a
mighty stream.
Amos 5:24

The Cleansing Rock

I knew the river
as my friend,
I knew each hole,
I knew each bend . . .
And it knew me
almost as well
Except for things
I couldn't tell . . .
But from this stream
I was to know;
it, too, had mud
within its flow . . .
And blessing not
the passing flock,
it cleansed itself
upon the rock . . .
"Oh, is there not
for me a Rock"
thought I, "my soul to mend?"
And God reveal'd
His precious Son . . .
My Saviour and my Friend.

There is none holy as the Lord: there is none beside
thee: neither is there any rock like our God.

I Samuel 2:2

Metaphor of Life

My foolish heart was touch'd with grief
when I beheld the tree
so terr'bly bent by nature's force
I question'd: Why would He,
Creator of all nature's realm,
not lift a helping hand?
His Spirit answered: Foolish mind,
that tree will surely stand . . .
For with My testing comes its strength,
each root gains deeper hold.
I've made so many trees before,
think now I've lost the mold?
The tree of life is much the same,
each man must face his storm,
and through the strength of Jesus Christ
emerge in Godly form.

I can do all things through Christ which strengtheneth
me.   *Philippians 4:13*

The Trial of Faith

The trial of faith, though often hard,
   is never without reason;
For God permits each one his cross
   to bear but for a season . . .
And those who stand unmarred by pain,
   unite in fervent prayer;
That soon the vic'try of your faith
   will banish ev'ry care.

That the trial of your faith, being much more precious
than of gold that perisheth, though it be tried with
fire, might be found unto praise and honour and glory
at the appearing of Jesus Christ.   *I Peter 1:7*

The Gentle Touch

The sooner we learn
to ably discern
the Voice of the Holy Ghost,
the better we'll know
to come and to go
that we might achieve the most . . .
For the Spirit will lead
and determine the way;
He desires us to prosper so much!
The small Voice is still
and follows our will
for His is a gentle touch.

Unto you, O men, I call; and my voice is to the sons
of man.   *Proverbs 8:4*

Completed Love

To love the lovely is no task,
   With ease the cause is render'd . . .
But loving those whom we oppose
   Need hearts by God's love tender'd . .
And love accomplished in the mind
   Is merely but a start . . .
For minds of men can soon be chang'd
   But God must change the heart . . .
And once the heart has gain'd repose,
   The Spirit like a dove
Glides gently through the human door
   Replacing hate with love.

Let love be without dissimulation . . .   *Romans 12:9*

Abundant Living

Though my heart has been your purchase,
I have lacked the strength Divine,
for what Thou hast intended,
I've not received as mine . . .
Oh the sin that I've committed,
although I'd often heard,
is the sin of not believing
each facet of His word . . .
In the wake of God's great trumpet,
I repent of foolish pride,
and receive the great abundance
for which He truly died.

The Spirit itself beareth witness with our spirit, that we are the children of God: And if children, then heirs; heirs of God, and joint heirs with Christ; if so be that we suffer with him, that we may be also glorified together. *Romans 8: 16 & 17*

Rejoice

Rejoice when hills that loom ahead
   Grow steeper by the hour . . .
For we climb not in our own strength,
   But by His regal power . . .
Assail the path with greater stride,
   Rejoice in greater height!
For we who walk within His steps,
   Acquire His matchless might.

Let the heart of them rejoice that seek the Lord. Seek
the Lord and his strength, seek his face continually.
I Chronicles 16:10, 11

God's Secret Weapon

The die was cast, its mold made known,
   Rebellion's seed had now been sown,
And one of three with trem'bling voice
   Renounced the Lord by willful choice . . .

"Just follow me" came Satan's cry,
   "A better life" became his lie,
And thinking he should mount the Throne,
   Assumed the Crown his very own . . .

This evil one with selfish eye
   Knew not a God whose Son would die,
A God whose Son might suffer loss
   That we might gain beneath His cross . . .

Incredible! What joy divine
   That One would bear this shame of mine!
A secret once for ages seal'd
   God's weapon LOVE, at last reveal'd . . .

But we speak the wisdom of God in a mystery, even the hidden wisdom, which God ordained before the world unto our glory: Which none of the princes of this world knew: for had they known it, they would not have crucified the Lord of glory.

I Corinthians 2: 7, 8

The Stand of Faith

From sight and sound,
from taste and touch,
from senses stand aloof;
for faith stands on
the Word of God . . .
It needs no further proof.

. . . and this is the victory that overcometh the world,
even our faith.   *I John 5:4*

The Greatest Sin

Your sermon, sir, flung wide the gates
    Exposing darkest sin . . .
And I dare say one hesitates
    To criticize 'a win'. . .
But hear me out before you judge,
    Why did you not tell all?
The sin that God abhors the most
    Has plagued your very 'call'. . .
The countless sick, the hopeless rows,
    The evidence at large,
All points to faithless unbelief
    Establishing each charge . . .
The common sins of human flesh
    Were really all we heard . . .
The greatest sin was left untold . . .
    Not honoring God's Word!

Take heed, brethren, lest there be in any of you an
evil heart of unbelief, in departing from the living God.
                                          Hebrews 3:12

My Fragrant Garden

There is no sweeter essence
from those whom I've ador'd,
Than that sweet Holy Presence
of Jesus Christ, my Lord . . .
For His atoning pardon
from which I daily feed,
Becomes my fragrant garden
embracing ev'ry need . . .

. . . Let my beloved come into his garden, and eat his
pleasant fruits.   *The Song of Solomon 4:16*

Mountain Tops

Most people want their share of fame
with its attendant limelight . . .
and hazards near the mountain top
demand that people climb right.
But mountain tops with all their view
are usually capped with snow . . .
It's in the valley warm and green
that tender gardens grow.

In every thing give thanks: for this is the will of God
in Christ Jesus concerning you. *I Thessalonians 5:18*

Song of Eternal Life

Before the real melodic line
   unfolds its lovely theme,
A pattern first is introduced,
   a verse to stitch the seam . . .

And as the fragile strand of sound
   resolves into a chord,
The beauty of eternal song
   bursts forth now from the Lord . . .

Eternal life is much the same
   beginning here on earth;
The preparation for a work
   unknown in total worth . . .

But God who plans each step we take
   considers not a fall,
For whom He takes back to the throne
   is ready for His call . . .

The introduction and the verse
   must serve its mortal place,
But greater song hath no man sung
   than that enrich'd by grace . . .

Let every man abide in the same calling wherein he
was called.   *I Corinthians 7:20*

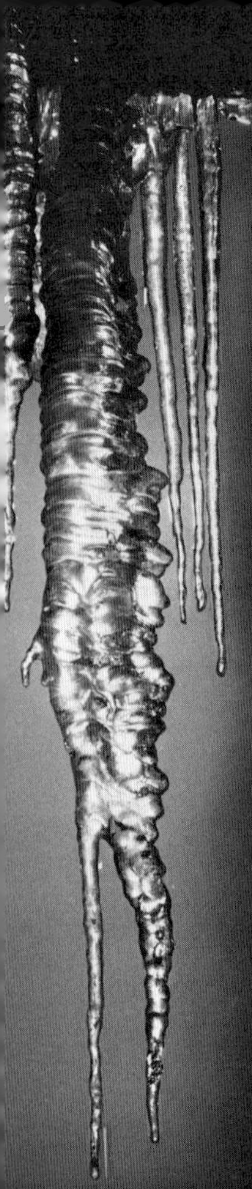

Confession

I knew the day
would go this way;
I knew it from the start . . .
How often men
have made this quote
and made it from the heart . . .
It's not just mere
coincidence;
it's far more than a guess . . .
The day will go
the way you SAY;
we ARE what we confess.

. . . we are more than conquerors,
through him that loved us.
Romans 8:37

Peaceful Rest

The will of man that none should die
    lies deeply in us all;
Yet wisdom speaks, and in its cry
    we hear the Father's call:
"Come hither now to higher ground
    that you might have my best,
And suffer not the raging storm . . .
    For you, I've offered rest."

Precious in the sight of the Lord
is the death of his saints.
Psalm 116: 15

In Him, no fearful sound

Since ALL things work together for good
For those who are led of the Spirit,
The thunderous roar brings only the rain
And rejoicing to those who doth hear it.

A merry heart doeth good like medicine . . .

Proverbs 17:22

Portrait of Faith

O wretched man! Futility
has cursed your ev'ry care.
Ten thousand times the strength of man
could not your burden bear.
The rattle of the serpent's tail
has issued death's corsage,
But wretched man, all is not lost!
Faith honors not mirage.
For what appears as hopelessness
has not been painted well;
For on the canvas fear has wrought
appears the mark of hell.
Both death and hell cannot prevail
when touch'd by matchless grace;
For from the Throne, the Sun has shone
that we might see His face.

But unto you that fear my name shall the Sun of
righteousness arise with healing in his wings . . .

Malachi 4:2

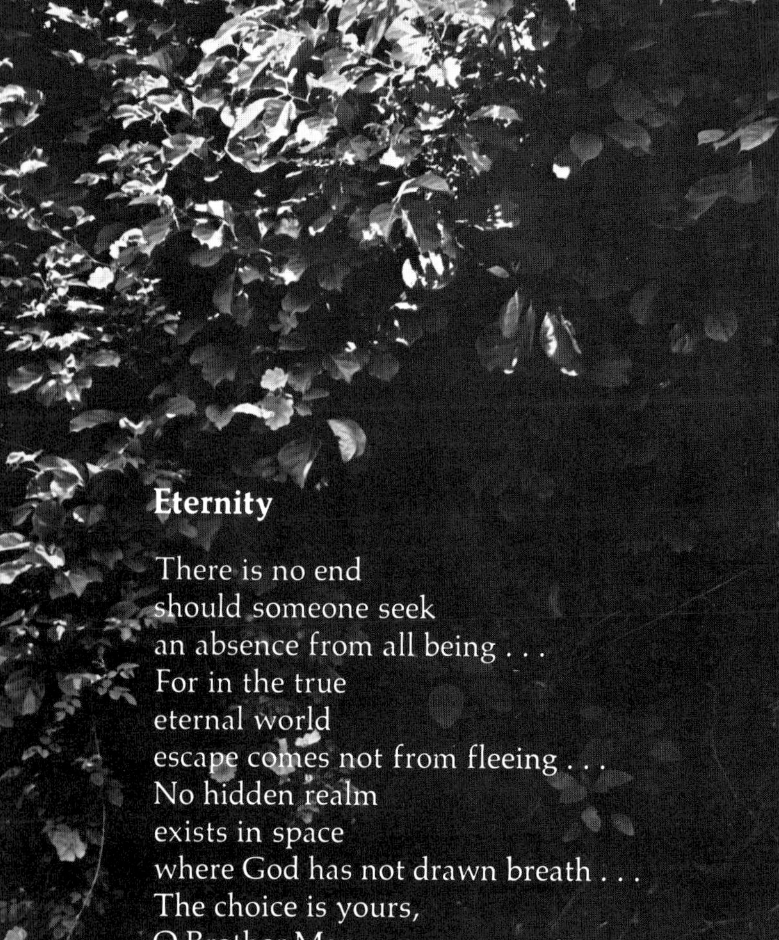

Eternity

There is no end
should someone seek
an absence from all being . . .
For in the true
eternal world
escape comes not from fleeing . . .
No hidden realm
exists in space
where God has not drawn breath . . .
The choice is yours,
O Brother Man,
eternal life or death.

And this is the record, that God hath given to us
eternal life, and this life is in His Son. - *I John 5:11*

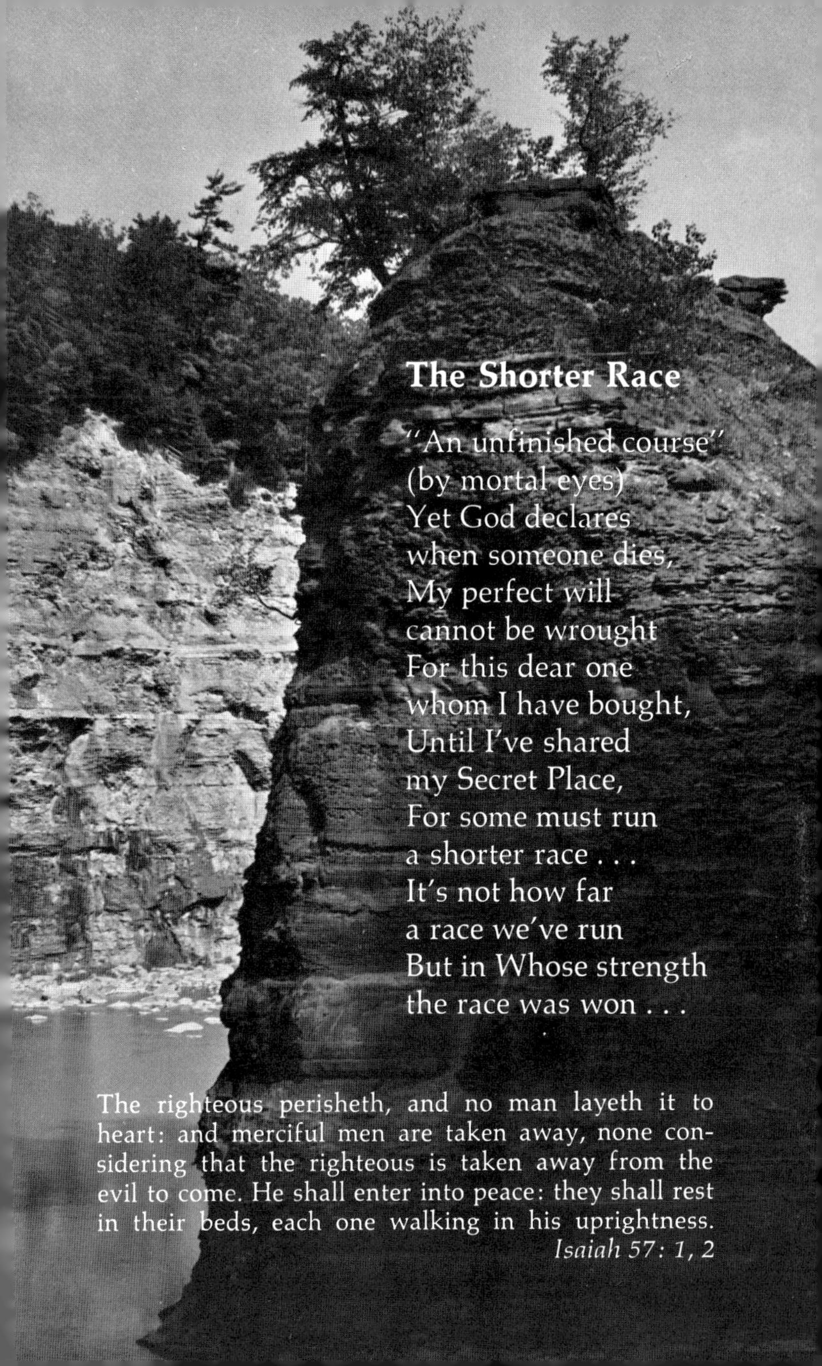

The Shorter Race

"An unfinished course"
(by mortal eyes)
Yet God declares
when someone dies,
My perfect will
cannot be wrought
For this dear one
whom I have bought,
Until I've shared
my Secret Place,
For some must run
a shorter race . . .
It's not how far
a race we've run
But in Whose strength
the race was won . . .

The righteous perisheth, and no man layeth it to heart: and merciful men are taken away, none considering that the righteous is taken away from the evil to come. He shall enter into peace: they shall rest in their beds, each one walking in his uprightness.
Isaiah 57 : 1, 2

The Noble Quest

The cautious seldom suffer loss
    Nor entertain despair . . .
The valiant knowing well the cost
    Proceed, yet well aware
That forces lurking to destroy
    Might end the noble quest . . .
But life is only worth its while
    When man has done his best.

Through God we shall do valiantly: for he it is that shall tread down our enemies. *Psalm 60:12*

Fame

I dare not say that seeking fame
is more or less a virtue . . .
It's your reaction to your name
that will or will not hurt you.

Pride goeth before destruction, and an haughty spirit
before a fall.   *Proverbs 16:18*

Perfected Life

The "keeping up", the "surge ahead",
the unrelenting fears
that man may not perfect his course
within the fleeting years . . .
The simple truth (yet so profound)
is found in nature's lair . . .
Perfected life is gained with ease
when cradled in His care.

And yet I say unto you,
That even Solomon in all
his glory was not arrayed
like one of these.
Matthew 6:29